COLOUR CLOSE-UP

WORLD WAR II ALLIED VEHICLES

COLOUR CLOSE-UP

WORLD WAR II ALLIED VEHICLES

Jan Suermondt

The Crowood Press

First published in 2001 by
The Crowood Press Ltd
Ramsbury, Marlborough
Wiltshire SN8 2HR

British Library Cataloguing-in-Publication Data
A catalogue record for this book is available from
the British Library

ISBN 1 86126 417 8

Edited by Martin Windrow
Designed by Tony Stocks/Compendium
Printed and bound in Singapore by Craft Print

Author's note

This book obviously does not offer anything approaching a
comprehensive guide to the Allied vehicles of World War II;
rather, it aims to provide - together with a companion volume on
Axis vehicles now in preparation - a detailed look at a
representative cross-section of such vehicles. It is also unusual
in that, through the use of an analytical approach to photography,
a much more detailed source of visual reference has been created
than is the norm. A decision was made early on to include
interiors where possible, and to provide close-up shots of some of
the more interesting details.

The selection of subjects may at first appear somewhat
arbitrary, but was dictated to some degree by the availability of
preserved examples suitable for photography. I apologise in
advance to any readers who feel that there are glaring omissions;
depending upon the reception of this book I shall endeavour to
produce additional volumes to fill some of the gaps. I have
included some vehicles which were not completely restored and
refinished, in order not to omit some interesting subjects; and
the practical factors governing the use of preserved vehicles on
today's roads often made the inclusion of civilian number plates
unavoidable. For similar reasons a few other post-war details
will be spotted by the sharp-eyed: some vehicles have exhibitors'
tickets displayed on the windscreen; the Dodge ambulance has an
inaccurate rear towing-ball, and the Mack NO added modern wing
mirrors; some of the Browning M2 .50cal machine guns have been
converted for 'firing' effects, and have a black compressed air hose
leading down into their mountings.

In addition to the vehicles themselves, I have taken the
opportunity to include photographs of some associated pieces of
heavy equipment - in this volume, a few of the artillery pieces
which were routinely towed by the vehicles featured. To include
mention of these in the book's title might have been pedantically
correct but would have given a false impression, so readers are
invited to regard them as a bonus. There are a number of ways in
which the sequence of subjects covered here could have been
arranged - by broad categories, and/or by nationality - but for
the sake of simplicity I chose more or less alphabetical order.

Many thanks are owed to all those vehicle owners and restorers
whose blood, sweat and tears have gone into preserving these
vehicles and without whom this book would not have been possible.

CONTENTS

Austin K5
Truck, 3-ton, 4x4, General Service

Large numbers of British 3-ton 4x4s were produced during the war, the majority by Bedford (a division of Vauxhall Motors), Ford and Austin. The Austin vehicle, the K5, was developed to fulfil a specification issued by the War Office in 1939. It entered production in 1941, and by the end of the war 12,280 had been manufactured, making it the second most numerous of the British four-wheel-drive trucks after the Bedford QL.

All K5s apart from the early production K5 YN models had removable cab tops to reduce their overall height for shipping. The K5 chassis was fitted with a variety of bodies, including the general service, anti-tank portee, cipher office, machinery, and wireless. The AT portee was fitted with a half cab and carried a complete 6-pounder anti-tank gun on a flatbed body, though it could also be towed. The gun could be fired from its position on the truck; this arrangement had proved relatively successful in the open terrain of North Africa, where mobility was more important than concealment, but once the desert war ended there was

little prospect of using the portee in its intended role, and most were rebuilt with GS bodies.

The Austin K5 was fitted with a 6-cylinder petrol engine, producing 85bhp. Its dimensions were: length, 19ft 8ins; width, 7ft 3ins; height, 9ft 11ins, or 6ft 8ins with cab top and tilt removed. Weight was 3.75 tons.

The example shown carries the markings of the 2nd/4th Battalion, Hampshire Regiment, serving in 28th Infantry Brigade with 4th Infantry Division in 1944. The brown square with the white unit serial number '69' identified the junior of the three battalions in an infantry brigade. The divisional sign as used in 1944-45 showed a complete red disc on a white square, with one 'fourth' cut out; earlier a single red 'quadrant' had been used by 4th Division.

Bedford MWD
Truck, 15-cwt, 4x2, General Service

In 1935 Vauxhall Motors, the makers of Bedford trucks, were invited to take part in comparative trials of new designs being held by the War Office. In 1938 a more powerful engine was developed and fitted, and contingency plans were laid for series production. In August 1939 the first 50 Bedford 15-hundredweight trucks were ordered, all of which were to be portees for carrying the 2-pdr anti-tank gun. This was followed in September, on the outbreak of war, by a further order for 2,000 vehicles; of these 480 were portees and the remainder GS trucks. A few weeks later an order was placed for a further 11,000, and this was subsequently increased still further; the Bedford MW was eventually to make up a large proportion of the 250,000 vehicles built by Bedford during the war.

The basic GS truck, although intended as a transport vehicle for the infantry section, came to be widely used by all arms. Early production MWs had open cabs, folding 'aero' type windshields and canvas side screens, with a folding hood for bad weather. From 1943 a more enclosed cab was fitted, with side doors, a canvas top and perspex side screens providing better protection. Several special purpose bodies were fitted; these were termed the Portee, Water Tanker, Fitted For Wireless, Wireless House Type, and Tractor. The basic GS version, designated MWD, was fitted with a 6-cylinder petrol engine, producing 72bhp. Its dimensions were: length, 14ft 4.5ins; width, 6ft 6.5ins; height, 7ft 6ins (5ft 3ins with tilt and windshield folded). The weight was 2.25 tons.

This example has been decorated with both the British 2nd Army sign and the 'all-seeing eye' of the

Guards Armoured Division. The yellow plate bearing a black number indicates the vehicle's 'bridging weight' - it required bridges with a capacity of three tons. This was a vital factor in the combat zone, where many water and other obstacles were bridged by the military with temporary spans of limited capacity. In North-West Europe vehicles of all the Allied armies were supposed to carry the white star recognition sign.

Bedford OYD
Truck, 3-ton, 4x2, General Service

The 3-tonner was the backbone of British military transport during the war: numbers rose from around 10,000 in 1939 to almost 390,000 by VE-Day in May 1945. Practically all the major British truck manufacturers produced 3-ton 4x2 types, and large numbers were also supplied by Canada and the USA, both directly and via Lend-Lease. In May 1939, as part of the rapid prewar expansion programme, Vauxhall, producers of Bedford trucks, had been asked by the War Office to prepare a prototype 4x2 3-tonner based on their commercial model. The vehicle, suitably modified for military service, entered production later that year with an initial contract for 11,000 vehicles. This was subsequently greatly increased, and the Bedford OYD was to make up the majority of this class of vehicle in British service.

Early GS trucks had wooden bodies but later production vehicles had bodies of steel construction. A great many body types were mounted on this chassis, including those termed Battery Slave, Light Breakdown, Machinery, Petrol Tanker, Searchlight, Store, Tipping, Water Tanker, Mobile Canteen, Field Bakery, and Mobile Laboratory - to name but a few. Many Bedfords were also supplied to the USSR between 1941 and 1944. Vehicles in the British Army served in all British theatres of operations and continued in service for many years after the war. The Bedford OYD used a 6-cylinder petrol engine, producing 72bhp. Overall dimensions were: length, 20ft 5ins;

width, 7ft 1.5ins; height, 10ft 2ins, and the unladen weight was 2.65 tons. This example has been marked with a sign incorporating the unit serial number of one of the regiments of 4th Armoured Brigade within 7th Armoured Division, and the 2nd Army sign.

Bedford QL
Truck, 3-ton, 4x4, General Service

Bedford's interest in this type of vehicle went back to December 1938 when engineers working at Vauxhall (Bedford's parent company) suggested the feasibility of producing a four-wheel-drive Bedford. The advantages of an all-wheel-drive truck for military use were obvious, and the War Office were asked for permission to proceed with a design. The War Office, although interested, felt that the project should proceed only on a low-priority basis. Vauxhall were already engaged in the development of 4x2 trucks in the 15-cwt, 30-cwt and 3-ton categories and these were to be given priority. The outbreak of war provided new impetus, and Vauxhall were asked to commence construction of 4x4 prototypes as soon as possible. The detailed specification was approved by October 1939 and the first prototype was ready for trials on 1 February 1940. The trials were remarkably successful, and the vehicle was ordered into production in February 1941 under the Bedford designation QL. Production continued until the end of the war, by which time 52,245 had been built - a far higher total than for any other British vehicle of the war.

As well as the standard GS type body the QL was fitted with a wide variety of special body types, including a refuelling bowser for the RAF, a fire tender, a troop carrier, and a 'house' type body which was used for a variety of purposes - e.g. mobile canteens, mobile laboratories and dental surgeries for field hospitals, offices, radio trucks, and command vehicles. The QL was also employed as a tractor unit for the 6-ton GS semi-trailer. It was adapted for use as an anti-tank gun portee in North Africa; this modification involving the

fitting of a soft-top cab and the provision of a flat bed body on which a 6-pdr anti-tank gun was mounted.

The standard Bedford QL 4x4 GS was fitted with a 6-cylinder engine producing 72hp. Overall dimensions were: length, 19ft 8ins; width, 7ft 6ins; and height, 9 feet 10 inches. The example shown here is a standard GS finished in the markings of 827th Armoured Troops Workshop, Royal Electrical & Mechanical Engineers (REME), with 79th Armoured Division.

(Left) A troop carrier-bodied Bedford QLD; the white serial number '53' on red indicated a regiment within an armoured division or independent armoured brigade.

(Below) The Bedford QL also served as a tractor for the Bofors 40mm light anti-aircraft gun, for which role it was fitted with a special body with accommodation for the gun crew and lockers for ammunition, spare gun barrel and associated equipment. This QLB tractor is finished in the markings of 58th LAA Regiment, 11th Armoured Division. The number '73' on the Royal Artillery's red and blue flash identifies the regiment within the division; 'T3B' indicates the third vehicle, of B Troop, towed (as opposed to self-propelled). Permission to photo-graph the QLB tractor and Bofors gun was kindly granted by Mr I.Airey of Harwich, the owner and restoration team leader.

(Right) View through the right hand door of the QLB artillery tractor's crew cab.

(Below) Interior of the crew cab seen through the left hand door.

SIGHTS, 40MM AA GUN MOUNTING MARK 3.

BOX SPARE PARTS & IMPLEMENTS 40MM AA GUN MARK 2.

Bofors 40mm L/60 Light Anti-Aircraft Gun

The Bofors company of Sweden have designed many weapons, but in the context of World War II the Bofors name is synonymous with the 40mm L/60 automatic light anti-aircraft gun developed in 1929. This weapon has been used at one time or another by almost every army in the world and, in modified form, is still in production today. During the war British forces employed it as a towed and self-propelled weapon and in fixed mountings on board ships.

The Bofors fired from four-round clips at a rate of 120 rounds per minute. It had a maximum horizontal range of 10,800 yards, an effective ceiling of 5,000 feet, and fired a 2lb high explosive shell fitted with an impact fuse and tracer, which destroyed itself after seven seconds if it missed its target. Maximum elevation was 90 degrees, traverse 360 degrees, and weight in action was 3.75 tons. Early war guns were entirely manually operated and used open sights, but later models used power control and had predictors to improve accuracy.

(Once again, thanks to Mr I.Airey of Harwich, the owner and restoration team leader, for permission to photograph the Bofors gun.)

Chevrolet 1½-ton (YP-G-4112)
Truck, 1½-ton, 4x4, cargo, w/winch

Although trucks in this class had been pioneered by Marmon-Herrington, and were also produced by Dodge, International and GMC, by far the biggest manufacturer was Chevrolet. During the war Chevrolet produced a total of about 145,000 one-and-one-half ton all-wheel-drive military trucks, compared with about 6,530 from International and some 6,410 from Dodge. All of the many variants were fitted with enclosed cabs except for the M6 bomb truck, which was fitted with a soft-top cab and folding windscreen; and the airborne cargo truck, which was modified to enable it to be dismantled into three assemblies for transport inside the C-37 Skytrain (DC-3 Dakota) aircraft. Only a few of these latter were modified from standard trucks in 1944.

The Chevrolet 1½ ton chassis was produced in two main series: the G-4100, produced from 1940 to 1941, and the G-7100 from 1942 to 1945. It was fitted with a variety of bodies, including cargo with and without winch, cargo long wheelbase, panel, telephone maintenance, telephone pole auger, crash rescue, dumper with and without winch, bomb carrier, and airfield lighting. The truck was also supplied as a chassis/cab for special bodies. It was powered by a 6-cylinder engine, producing 93 horsepower; front wheel drive could be disengaged for road travel. The 1½ ton Chevrolet had a maximum speed of 48 miles per hour, and weighed 8 tons. Overall dimensions of the cargo-bodied truck were: length, 19ft 3ins; width, 7ft 2ins; height, 8ft 8.5ins (7ft 3ins without tilt).

Diamond T / Rogers Tank Transporter (M19)

Truck-trailer, 45-ton, tank transporter, comprising Truck, 12-ton, 6x4, prime mover, M20 (Diamond T 981); & trailer, M9 (Rogers Bros)

The Diamond T 12-ton prime mover M20 was originally designed in 1940 to meet the requirements of the British Purchasing Mission to the USA, who were placing orders with various firms to replace or supplement existing equipment. The Diamond T was ordered for use in conjunction with the 'trailer, M9, 45-ton, British Mk I', for the recovery and transport of tanks. This combination, known in the US under the designation 'truck-trailer, 45-ton, tank transporter, M19', was introduced in 1940/41. It first saw active service with the British Army in North Africa, where the conditions of war made the recovery of mechanical break-downs or combat-damaged tanks from the battlefield a vital consideration. The M19 was later also adopted for use by the US Army.

The Diamond T M20 was equipped with a 20-ton winch and a ballast body behind the cab. Early production vehicles had pressed steel cabs, but from August 1943 they were fitted with an open type cab and had provision for a ring-mounted anti-aircraft machine gun. There were two models, the 980 and the 981. The 980 had a 300ft winch cable and two winch cable roller sheaves at the rear; the 981 had a 500ft cable, three winch sheaves at the rear, and a roller assembly in the front bumper allowing the winch cable to be paid out to the front of the vehicle.

The Diamond T was a remarkably rugged vehicle; of almost unrivalled longevity, it served on in the British Army into the 1970s. It was also used by numerous heavy haulage firms for many years after the war. The Diamond T M20 weighed 25.8 tons and was powered by a Hercules DFXE 6-cylinder diesel engine, producing 185bhp; it had a cruising range of 300 miles. The overall dimensions were: length, 23ft 4ins; width, 8ft 5ins; height, 8 feet 5 inches. The usual crew was two men.

The trailer M9, British Mk I, was designed and built by Rogers Bros and was later also produced by four other manufacturers. It was rated to carry loads up to a maximum of 45 tons, and could thus shift all Allied AFVs up to and including the M4 Sherman series. Its overall dimensions were: length, 30ft; width, 9ft 6ins; height, 5 feet 2 inches.

Daimler Dingo Mk II Scout Car

The Dingo resulted from a 1938 War Office specification calling for a small vehicle with frontal armour of at least 25mm, capable of resisting infantry light anti-tank weapons and able to head a column of tanks or other vehicles likely to encounter opposition. The vehicle was to be armed with a .303in Bren light machine gun, and should be able to withdraw quickly in reverse; for this reason only frontal armour was specified in order to save weight.

Three companies submitted designs and these were tested in the latter half of 1938, the one from BSA (Birmingham Small Arms) being selected. During the development of the vehicle the War Office decided that the sides should also be armoured, the engine should be protected and an armoured roof should be added. The vehicle eventually entered service as the 'car, scout, Daimler Mk I', BSA having been bought out by Daimler in the meantime. It soon became more commonly known as the Dingo, the name originally given to the losing Alvis prototype. The Mk I cars all had four-wheel steering, but this was deleted in the Mk II as it caused difficulties for inexperienced drivers, and at high speeds could lead to the vehicle rolling over. The Dingo's gearbox had five speeds in forward and five in reverse to allow for a speedy withdrawal. The

driver's seat was turned inwards to enable him to look over his left shoulder when driving in reverse. The armoured roof was usually removed in service, and was deleted altogether from the Mk III. For better visibility a high external seat was often fitted for the commander.

The Dingo was one of the most effective vehicles of its type to be built and was widely used by the British and Commonwealth armies on all major fronts. It served in the reconnaissance troops of armoured regiments, with armoured car regiments, and as a liaison vehicle at every level. A total of 6,626 of all marks were produced, and the Dingo remained in service long after the war. The Mk II was powered by a Daimler 18HP 6-cylinder engine, producing 55 horsepower. The Dingo carried an armament of one .303in Bren LMG and a crew of two. Overall dimensions were: length, 10ft 5ins; width, 5ft 7.75ins; height, 4ft 11ins; with armour up to a maximum of 30mm thickness the laden weight was 3 tons.

This immaculately restored and stowed example carries the markings of a vehicle in B Squadron of the Westminster Dragoons, attached to the 79th Armoured Division.

(Opposite, above & right)
Right side details.

(Below) **Right rear details - note that the right rear suspension unit is painted white in order to reflect the convoy light, mounted under the vehicle for use in blackout conditions.**

(Opposite top) **Left rear, with 79th Armoured Division sign.**

(Opposite bottom) **Left side, with commander/ gunner's side access door open.**

Commander/gunner's left side access door, partially blocked by his seat pillar.

Left side details, including bolted-on rear stowage rack and observation seat, and pioneer tools.

Three-quarter front
views, with vision flaps
open and closed. Note
clamped-on 'sand chan-
nels' for use in 'soft
going'.

(Above) The Bren .303in light machine gun was quickly dismountable for ground use if the crew were forced to abandon the vehicle.

(Opposite top) Interior, looking forward. Note the generous supply of magazines racked beneath the Bren ahead of the commander/gunner's seat; and the 'toed-in' position of the driver's seat, to allow him to turn partly to his left when reversing at speed - a manoeuvre which represented the little Dingo's most effective defence.

(Opposite) Interior, looking backwards. Note the No.4 rifle stowed in clips above the radio set; and the difficult access to the commander/gunner's side door. In practice both crew normally went 'over the top' when entering or leaving the Dingo.

Dodge Ambulance (T214-WC54)

Truck, ³/₄-ton, 4x4, ambulance

From 1941 the US Army's ¹/₂-ton 4x4 range of vehicles as first introduced in 1936 was superseded by a new ³/₄-ton range. Prototypes were produced by Ford and Dodge, the latter becoming the large-scale producer of this type. The improved 1942 models were sturdier and wider, had a lower silhouette, and were fitted with high floatation combat tyres. They came in three wheelbase lengths - 98in, 114in and 121 inches. The first to see active service were 'weapons carriers' (open-cab pick-up style trucks) and ambulances supplied to the British Army in the North African desert.

In addition to the standard weapons carrier the ³/₄-ton WC series Dodges were supplied in a variety of body types including command car, radio car, closed cab pick-up, emergency repair and telephone installation trucks, a 'suburban' or 'carry-all', 37mm AT gun carrier, and panel vans of various applications. The

best-known of the latter was this field ambulance, with a steel panel body built by Wayne on a 121in wheelbase chassis. The T214-WC54 ambulance could carry four stretcher cases or seven seated casualties. It was used on every front by all arms of the US military and was also supplied to the Allies. Some 26,000 were built between 1942 and May 1944, and although replaced thereafter by the more easily shipped WC64 a number even soldiered on through the Korean War.

The Dodge ambulance was powered by a Dodge T214 6-cylinder engine producing 92 brake horsepower. It weighed 5.8 tons, and its overall dimensions were: length, 16ft 2.5ins; width, 6ft 5.75ins; height, 7 feet 6 inches. The example shown here represents a vehicle of the 63rd Medical Surgery Group of the US 3rd Army. The grey-painted ambulance on pages 46-47 carries the markings of a vehicle on the strength of the hospital at Ahwahnee US Navy station.

General Motors Corp. DUKW-353

Truck, 2½-ton, 6x6, amphibian

The 'Duck' (as it was invariably pronounced) was the result of a programme initiated in 1942 to develop a vehicle to ferry stores from ships lying offshore to dumps within a beachhead without the aid of port facilities. The DUKW amphibious truck utilised the chassis of the standard American COE type 2½ ton 6x6 truck (see pages 56-59), fitted with a barge-shaped body. It was designed by naval architects Sparkman & Stephens of New York in conjunction with the Yellow Truck & Bus Co., main producers of the 2½-ton truck (Yellow Truck & Bus Co. became the Truck & Coach Division of General Motors in 1943). The new hull incorporated buoyancy tanks, a screw propeller and a rudder. The propeller and wheels could be powered together for entering and leaving the water; and tyre pressure could be adjusted while running (see pages 52-53).

The trials of the pilot model were so successful that it was ordered into production at once, and was standardised in October of 1942. The DUKW was first used in action in the landings at Noumea in the Pacific in March 1943. Shortly after that DUKWs were used in the invasion of Sicily, and from then on they partic-

ipated in all amphibious operations in both the European and Pacific theatres of operations. In 1943, the first year of production, 4,508 vehicles were built; when production ceased in late 1945 the total had reached 21,247. DUKWs played an important part in the Normandy landings; though numbers were swamped and lost in the early hours of D-Day through being launched in choppy water too far off shore, they proved invaluable during the vital build-up phase of the campaign, when the bulk of stores still had to come ashore over the beaches for lack of operational port facilities. Its unique capabilities ensured that the DUKW would continue in service in a number of countries for many years after the war.

Its apt phonetic name was taken from its technical designation: D for 1942, the year of its design; U for utility; K indicating all-wheel-drive; and W, indicating dual rear axles. The DUKW had a capacity of 2½ tons or up to 50 men. It was 31ft long, 8ft 3ins wide and 8ft 8ins high with canopy raised (7ft 6ins with canopy lowered). Maximum speed was 5 knots at sea and 50 mph on land. It was sometimes fitted with a ring mount for an AA machine gun above the cab.

General Motors Corp. 2½-ton Truck (CCKW-353)

The 2½ ton 6x6 'light-heavy' truck was the most widely used tactical transport vehicle of the US forces in World War II; this 'Jimmy' or 'deuce-and-a-half' saw widespread service in all theatres. Over 800,000 were produced, the majority of them by GMC who built 562,750 examples. The first GMC 2½-ton 6x6 was basically an all-wheel-drive version of a commercial type, the ACKWX-353, which was also ordered by the French government. The familiar military pattern front end was introduced in 1941 when the vehicle was put into mass production, which proceeded at a phenomenal rate. By 1943 production at GMC was running continuously 24 hours a day, and a truck was rolling of the production line every four minutes.

There were two basic chassis models: the CCKW-352 with 145in wheelbase, and the CCKW-353 with 164in wheelbase. In 1943 the open cab became standard, to simplify production and save raw materials; many closed-cab trucks were later retro-converted to this standard. Some trucks were fitted with a ring mount for a .50cal machine gun above the cab, both for anti-aircraft use and to offer some defence in the event of an ambush, the operator standing up on the passenger's seat to fire the gun.

The standard cargo trucks were equipped with one of three basic body types: all steel; steel-sided with a wooden floor; or all wood. All three types had fold-down bench seats in the rear that could accommodate 16 combat-equipped troops or could be folded up to make way for cargo. In addition to the standard cargo body the 2½-ton chassis was fitted with a multitude of specialist bodies including bomb service, dumper, stock rack, tanker for gasoline or water, and high-lift cargo (for servicing aircraft). Van-type bodies were also fitted and these were equipped for a variety of special purposes, e.g. mobile workshops, blood banks, artillery repair workshops and communications. Many were delivered to the government with no body at all, and were later completed as required with one of these specialised bodies.

Serving on through the Korean War, the 'Jimmy' was not retired from service in the US Army until 1956. During and after World War II the US government supplied thousands of these trucks to Britain, Germany, France, the Netherlands, Argentina, Norway and other smaller countries; it was not until 1985 that the French Army disposed of the last 5,000 in their inventory. As a result, many trucks still survive across Europe in very good condition.

The CCKW-353 truck had a GMC 270 engine generating 104 brake horsepower; it had a maximum speed of 45mph and weighed 5.175 tons. The front axle could be disengaged for road travel. Overall dimensions were: length, 21ft 4.25ins; width, 7ft 4ins; height, 9 feet 2 inches. The examples illustrated here are **(above & opposite top)** a short wheelbase cargo with a hard-top cab, machine gun ring mount and front winch; **(opposite, & page 58 top)** a long wheelbase cargo with soft-top cab; and **(page 58 bottom & page 59)** a gasoline tanker.

Harley-Davidson WLA 1939

Motorcycle, solo

The WLA was a standard production machine, adapted for military service. The modifications included the fitting of a rear carry rack, leather panniers, front and rear crash bars, a windscreen, a scabbard for a Thompson sub-machine gun or rifle on the right front fork leg, and a crank case guard; and the application of an all-over service livery with a black exhaust system. The big Harley stood up admirably to the rigours of military use; it was standard practice to drop the bike on its side in certain situations, and bikes serving in armoured divisions were sometimes transported lashed to the engine decks of the tanks. That neither of these practices seemed to have any detrimental effect is a testament to their rugged construction and reliability.

The WLA was successful and well-liked in service, being used for solo despatch, escort, convoy control and military police duties. Their effectiveness was reflected in their production figures, over 89,000 being built in the period 1939-44. Of these around 60,000 went to the US forces, and the majority of the remainder went to the British and Commonwealth armies, where they continued in use until the late 1950s.

The Harley-Davidson WLA was fitted with a Harley-Davidson 740cc sv V-twin engine, producing 23hp; maximum speed was 60 miles per hour. The overall dimensions were: length, 7ft 4ins; width, 3ft 0.25in; height, 3ft 5ins; and the bike weighed 575lbs loaded. The example illustrated lacks the windscreen.

Jeep
Truck, ¼-ton, 4x4, utility (Willys MB, Ford GPW)

The concept of a light military reconnaissance car was first formulated in the late 1930s, and this led to a formal requirement from the US Army. In the summer of 1940 Karl K.Probst of the Bantam Car Co. designed a vehicle to meet the US Army requirements, and a prototype was constructed. A further 70 examples of an improved model followed and were purchased by the US Ordnance Department for testing. The trial vehicles performed well and the Ordnance Department decided to purchase a further 1,500 cars. Their request to do so, however, was blocked by the Quartermaster General on the grounds that Bantam's production facilities were too limited to fulfil the order.

Two other manufacturers, Ford and Willys-Overland, had also been developing prototypes to meet the Army requirement. In spite of the fact that neither had been completed by the time the Bantam was tested, all three companies received contracts on completion of their respective prototypes to produce 1,500

vehicles, much to the annoyance of Bantam. These vehicles - known as the Bantam 40BRC, Willys MA and Ford GP - were subjected to further tests. These revealed that all three vehicles needed minor improvements but overall the Willys design was judged to be the best, and a production contract was awarded to Willys for 16,000 vehicles. After the suggested modifications had been made the new design, known as the Willys MB, entered production in December 1941. With a rapid increase in orders, demand soon outstripped Willys' production capabilities, and in early 1942 Ford were brought in to build vehicles to the Willys pattern. The Ford-built vehicle was identical in all but minor details and was known as the Ford GPW.

Most of the earlier models, although not of the finalised designs, were released for Lend-Lease and shipped to Britain, Russia and the Far East. Production of the standardised models, the GPW and the MB, reached a total of 639,245 by the end of the war: 361,349 MBs built by Willys-Overland, and

277,896 GPWs built by Ford. These vehicles were the first to be officially known as 'jeeps', the name purportedly being derived from GP - the abbreviation of 'general purpose'.

Apart from its original and basic role as a front-line reconnaissance and liaison vehicle, the rugged, endlessly versatile Jeep was extensively used for a huge variety of purposes on every front by all the Allied nations. Its small size and light weight fitted it to become the main air-portable transport vehicle for the airborne forces, towing 6pdr anti-tank guns, 75mm pack howitzers or ¹/₂-ton trailers. Its ability to get right forward over rough terrain led to it being widely used as a front-line ambulance, carrying two, three or even four stretchers. Fitted with flanged wheels, it ran on railway tracks in areas with few roads, especially in the Far East. Heavily armed with up to four machine guns, Jeeps were used as combat vehicles in North Africa, Italy and North-West Europe by the British SAS and other special forces, and at the end of the war some were fitted with

the newly introduced 'recoilless rifle' weapons. It was the most ubiquitous and popular Allied military vehicle of the war, and was still to be seen in service around the world for decades afterwards.

The standard Jeep was powered by a 4-cylinder Go Devil petrol engine producing 54bhp, and giving a 50mph maximum speed. Overall dimensions were: length, 11ft; width, 5ft 2ins; height, 6ft with the hood erected, 4ft 6ins with hood down and windscreen folded. Its unladen weight was 2,450 pounds.

The example shown here, fitted with a radio and a .50cal M2 Browning heavy machine gun, is marked as a vehicle of the 82nd Cavalry Reconnaissance Squadron of the US Army's 2nd Armored Division. Each of a squadron's three troops had 18 Jeeps and 12 M8 Greyhound armoured cars (see pages 93-97), plus a Stuart light tank troop (see pages 82-92) and a self-propelled howitzer troop.

'FIRE EATER'

AN/GRC-9
MT-350

(Pages 67-68) A Jeep finished as a vehicle of the British 79th Armoured Division; the serial '1235' on a blue flash identifies 42nd Assault Regiment, Royal Engineers.

LVT(A)-4 Alligator

One of a long line of 'Landing Vehicles, Tracked' born of America's rapid development of amphibious warfare techniques and equipment, the LVT (Armored)-4 entered production in 1943, and a total of 1,890 were built. The LVT series started with the original Alligator, designed by Donald Roebling Jr for use as a civilian rescue vehicle in the swamps of the Florida Everglades. The vehicle was redesigned for military service at the request of the USMC in 1940, and the first, unarmoured model was placed in production in November of that year. Its initial task was putting men and matériel ashore during assault landings on Pacific islands; its tracks allowed it to cross lagoon reefs which hampered the approach of conventional landing craft.

The costly landings on Tarawa in November 1943 demonstrated that the LVT 'Amtracks' needed both armour protection and increased means of hitting back at the enemy. Although it was never designed as a combat vehicle and was generally unsuitable for that role, it was believed that an armoured, up-gunned LVT could usefully provide limited fire support for infantry during beach assaults until conventional tanks could be brought ashore. To this end a number of LVTs were provided with an armoured, fully enclosed hull on which was mounted the turret of the M3 Stuart light tank. This LVT(A)-1 also had two machine gun positions cut in the rear decking, each with a 30cal. MG on a ring mount, and a third was carried in the hull front.

The ability of these 'Amtanks' to accompany the infantry to the shore - returning the fire of Japanese positions, crossing reefs and traversing surf before continuing inland from the beach under fire - made them invaluable in the island-hopping campaigns of the Pacific theatre, and they were used extensively by both the US Army and Marines. In March 1944 it was decided that a heavier weapon was needed, and a successor to the LVT(A)-1 was designed. The new LVT(A)-4 had a similar hull to the LVT(A)-1 but mounted the turret and 75mm howitzer of the M8 Gun Motor Carriage; the two rear deck MG positions were deleted to offset the greater weight of the new turret. As well as serving in the Pacific, LVT(A)-4s were also to see action in northern Italy and in the crossing of the Rhine. After 1949 they were among the LVTs provided to the French Army fighting the 1946-54 Indochina War, and saw active service in swamp and coastal regions of Vietnam with amphibious units of the Foreign Legion armoured cavalry.

Weighing 18.3 tons, the LVT(A)-4 was 26ft 2ins long, 10ft 8ins wide and 10ft 2ins high. Armour protection was to a maximum of 13mm on the hull and 44mm on the turret, and the vehicle carried a crew of six. Power was provided by a 250bhp Continental engine giving a maximum speed of 16mph on land and 7mph on water; the vehicle was propelled through the water by the tracks, which were fitted with special 'W'-shaped grousers. Range was 150 miles on land and 100 miles in water. Armament consisted of one 75mm M2 or M3 howitzer, one hull-mounted .50cal Browning machine gun and sometimes a second .50cal MG on a mount at the turret rear. The vehicle illustrated here bears the markings of a US Army 'Amtank' unit - which were actually more numerous than those of the US Marine Corps.

(Opposite) Bow and forward superstructure.

(Opposite below) Rear deck, looking to the rear.

(Right) Forward superstructure, right side.

(Below) Forward superstructure, looking forward on right side.

CR-52S

S.R. 13S7S-I
ARMY ORDER 5042A

INSTA
IN HU
ATTEN

CDS
WT-33S23
CU-2SS6

M3 Series Half-Track Personnel Carrier

During the late 1930s the US Army made a request for a scout vehicle and artillery tractor with good cross-country performance. It was decided to take, as the basis of the new vehicle, the four-wheeled M3 Scout Car already being produced for the Army by the White Motor Company. The chassis and body of the scout car were modified to accept track units in place of the rear wheels. These track units were of a Kegresse type design, first employed on the Marmon-Herrington M2 half-track of 1937, and were adopted virtually unchanged for the new vehicle. Development of the new half-track was reasonably straightforward, combining as it did components of two existing vehicles. The design of the new vehicle was standardised as the Half-Track Armored Car M2 in September 1942, as was the similar but not identical Half-Track Personnel Carrier M3.

The M2 was designed to carry up to ten men, though in practice this was optimistic; it lacked a rear hull door, and its machine gun armament - one .50cal and one or two .30cal guns - was mounted on a slide rail around the inside upper edge of the hull. It was mainly used in various non-infantry roles. The longer-bodied M3 had an official capacity of 13 men, and a central rear door; in practice it could carry a ten-man infantry squad. The M3 was armed with a .30cal or .50cal machine gun on a central pedestal mount; in the M3A1 this was replaced by a ring mount in an armoured 'pulpit' above the front passenger seat, almost invariably mounting a .50cal gun.

The layout of the M3 was typical of the great majority of US half-tracks built during the war. The engine was in the conventional truck position and the transmission was led, via a transfer box, forward to the front wheels and back to the track drive wheels at the front of the track units. The track assembly consisted of four road wheels in a single bogie each side, a rear idler, a small return roller and the drive sprocket. The tracks were continuous rubber bands moulded around steel cable reinforcement, with steel bar grips for traction and metal track guides. On good surfaces the front axle drive was disengaged, power being provided through the tracks alone; for rough cross-country driving both units were powered. Some vehicles carried a sprung roller on the front bumper to help prevent the front wheels 'ditching'; this was increasingly replaced by a heavy frame mounting a winch.

The M2/M3 half-track series were used by the US forces in most theatres of war, and many were also supplied to America's allies, the majority to Britain, Canada and the USSR. Apart from providing the personnel transport for mechanised infantry units within the Allied armoured divisions, these versatile vehicles were also used as the basis for numerous variations including mortar carriers, multiple anti-aircraft guns, gun motor carriages, ambulances and others, totalling almost 70 variants. Many vehicles were also modified or retro-manufactured to fulfil particular roles or to up-date them to the latest standards - exact identification of a particular vehicle can be complex. The M2 and M3 were built by Autocar, Diamond T and White; International produced the M5 and M9 which were similar but for the fitting of their own engines and running gear. In all, including variants, production totalled 41,170 vehicles, mainly in the period 1941-44. They served on with a number of armies postwar, and were still in front-line service with the Israeli Defence Force into the 1970s.

The M3 was powered by a White 160AX 6-cylinder petrol engine, producing 147bhp; maximum speed was 45mph, and the vehicle weighed 8 tons unladen. Maximum armour thickness was 12.7mm, giving protection from small arms and shrapnel only. Overall dimensions were: length, 20ft 2.5ins; width, 6ft 5.5ins; height, 7ft 5ins (M3A1 with 'pulpit', 8ft 4ins).

M3 37mm Anti-Tank Gun

Often seen towed by M2 half-tracks, the M3 37mm was the standard American anti-tank gun when war broke out in Europe; but by the time of US entry into the war weapons of this calibre were largely ineffective in this theatre. The increasing thickness of tank armour in Europe rendered them all but impervious to the 37mm calibre/ 2-pounder weapons with which most armies had started the war. In the Pacific, however, it was a different story: the obsolete Japanese tanks were comparatively lightly armoured and were still vulnerable to the 37mm. The gun was also found to be extremely effective at breaking up Japanese infantry charges when provided with anti-personnel canister shot, and was used extensively in this role. Its light weight and easy manoeuvrability made it particularly useful in the Pacific campaigns.

The M3 weighed 990lb in action and fired a 2lb shell to a maximum range of 12,850 yards. Maximum elevation was 15 degrees and traverse was 60 degrees.

M3A1 Stuart Light Tank

In the 1930s a series of experimental combat cars and light tanks were produced for the US Army, culminating in the M2A4 which entered production in April 1940, a total of 365 eventually being built. Analysis of the war in France that year revealed the need for improvements. Armour protection was increased and the hull was lengthened to cover the exhausts. In order to support the increased weight and lengthened hull it was decided to adopt the distinctive trailing idler wheel that was to become characteristic of the Stuart series. The new vehicle was powered by a Wright Continental W-970-9A radial 7-cylinder air-cooled petrol aero engine, and was designated M3.

The original M3 was, like its predecessors, of all-riveted construction, although a welded turret was soon introduced to save weight and this in turn was replaced by a partly cast turret. At this stage a gyroscopic gun stabiliser was also fitted for the first time. Some late production M3s were powered by Guiberson diesel engines and had hulls of welded construction. The M3 entered production in mid-1941, and 5,811 were built before it was superseded by the next model in August 1942.

With the passing of the Lend-Lease Act in March 1941 supplies of the M3 began to reach Britain, where it first acquired the name Stuart, the Continental-engined vehicles being designated Stuart I and the diesels Stuart II (US-supplied tanks were all named after Civil War generals, and in time these British-bestowed names were adopted by the Americans). Despite its relatively thin armour and small 37mm gun, its high speed, mechanical reliability and excellent handling made it a suitable substitute for the British 'Cruiser' tanks, and it was soon in action in North Africa. The turn of 1941-42 saw US M3s in battle against the Japanese invaders of the Philippines, and it would soon prove itself on Guadalcanal.

Combat experience revealed the need for further modifications, and these were incorporated in the M3A1 model which entered production in June 1942; petrol- and diesel-powered M3A1s were known in Britain as the Stuart III and Stuart IV respectively (though the whole series was nicknamed by the Tommies themselves, who loved its speed and manoeuvrability, as the 'Honey'). The improvements included the fitting of a power traverse to the turret, the provision of a turret 'basket' floor, the deletion of the prominent commander's cupola, and the fitting of two turret hatches. Most M3A1s had the two sponson-mounted machine guns of the M3 deleted - they took up precious space in the already cramped interior and were of little practical value.

Production of the M3A1 totalled 4,600 Continental-engined examples and 211 Guiberson-powered vehicles by the time it was succeeded on the production lines in February 1943 by the M3A3 and the M5. Total production of the M3 series, including the M3A3, was 13,859 tanks. The Stuart series was also supplied to the Soviet, Australian, Indian, French and Chinese armies and to Marshal Tito's Yugoslav partisans, serving in every major theatre of war.

The M3A1 was powered by either a Wright Continental radial air-cooled 250bhp petrol or a Guiberson radial air-cooled 220bhp diesel engine; in either case the maximum road speed was 36 miles per hour. Armament consisted of a 37mm main gun and three .30cal machine guns, one mounted in the hull front, one co-axial with the main gun and one pintle-mounted outside the turret. Armour protection was to a maximum of 43mm, and the overall dimensions were: length, 14ft 10.75ins; width, 7ft 4ins; height, 7 feet 6.5 inches. The example shown carries the markings of Co.A of the 66th Armored Regiment, US 2nd Armored Division, in 1942.

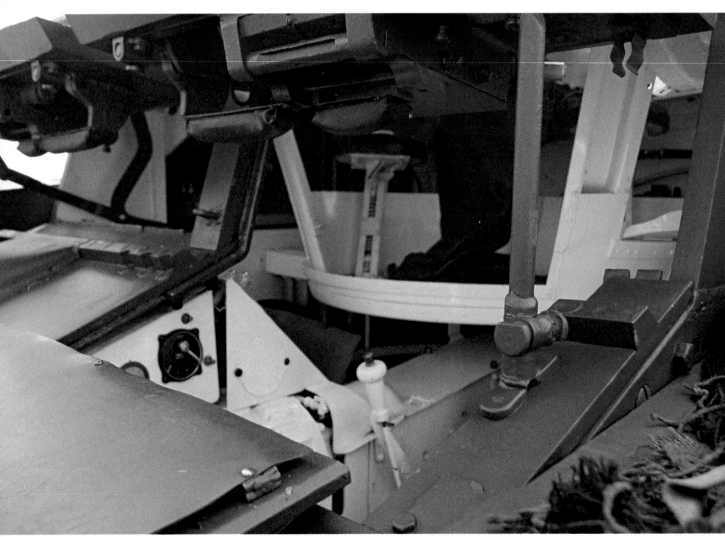

The Stuart carried a crew of only four; the driver and the co-driver/hull gunner/radio operator had fairly comfortable stations, but in the cramped little turret the commander was obliged to double as the main gun loader. In the M3A3 and M5 models the radio was also moved to the turret, adding yet another task to distract him.

(Left) Looking down through the turret basket from the commander's seat, forward and left to the driver's position.

(Below) Looking forward from the gunner's seat on the left side of the 37mm main gun. His periscope is at top left; the red-painted handle combines the power traverse control and firing triggers for the 37mm and co-axial machine gun; the elevation wheel is at bottom centre.

(Opposite) Looking down through the commander's hatch. Note the gunner's (left) and commander's (right) seats; the stowed Thompson SMG; the back-up manual turret traverse (bottom centre), and the traverse scale painted round the inside of the turret ring. The main gun breech is hidden here by a tarpaulin; below it the driver's compartment can just be seen.

(Opposite below) The turret interior, looking down and right from the gunner's hatch.

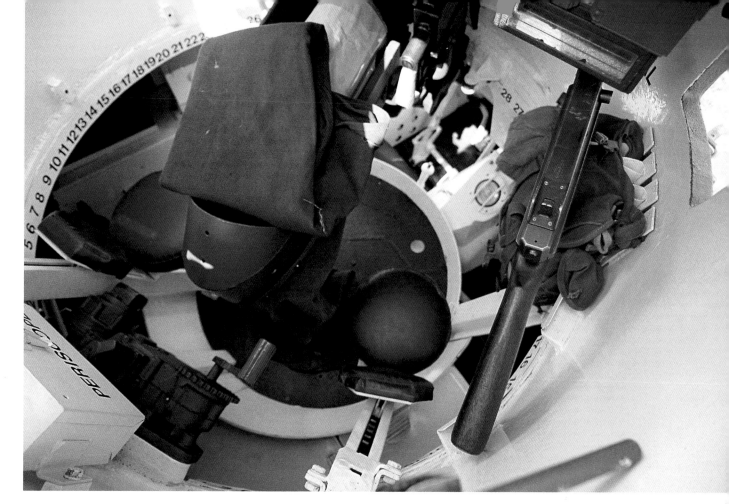

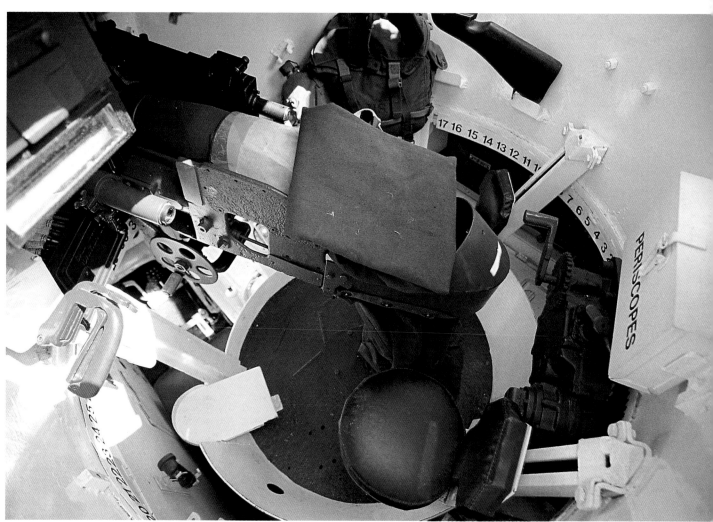

M5 Stuart Light Tank

The M5 development of the Stuart tank arose from a claim by the Cadillac division of General Motors that twin V-8 Cadillac car engines could be used in place of the M3's standard Wright Continental. A shortage of this power plant been caused by increased demand for these radial engines for aircraft production, and there were not sufficient Guiberson diesels to make up the shortfall. To test Cadillac's claim an M3E2 prototype was fitted with the twin V-8, together with Cadillac's Hydra-Matic automatic transmission; and after this successfully completed a 500-mile proving run the vehicle was ordered into production as the M5. Although the new tank retained the basic chassis and suspension of the M3 the opportunity was taken to completely redesign the hull. The new design was of improved ballistic shape, offered more space internally, and eased production due to its simpler shape. Maximum armour thickness was increased to 67mm; and although this resulted in an increase in weight of 4.3 tons over the M3 to 16.5 tons, the additional power of the new engine and the efficiency of the Cadillac transmission kept the maximum road speed at 36 miles per hour.

The M5 entered production in March 1942, and in August an M3A3 prototype appeared with a similar hull front shape to the M5. The new vehicle had the radio relocated to the turret, which was extended at the rear to accommodate it, and stowage and fuel capacity were both increased. This was followed a month later by the prototype M5A1 which incorporated all these refinements. In December both the Continental-powered M3A3 and the Cadillac-powered M5A1 were put into production. The M5A1 was soon found to be a generally superior vehicle to the M3A3, with its more flexible power plant and automatic transmission, and in August 1943 production of the M3A3 was halted in favour of the M5A1 after a total of 3,427 had been produced. Production of the M5A1 continued until June 1944 by which time 6,810 had been built. Total production of all M5 models was 8,884. The M5 series was supplied to Britain, where both M5 and M5A1 were known as Stuart VI.

The M5's two Cadillac V-8 petrol engines each produced 121bhp. The automatic transmission gave rapid acceleration, but the engines were surprisingly quiet - both factors appreciated by the crews. This was especially true in the reconnaissance units to which the now seriously out-gunned Stuart was increasingly relegated in Europe from 1943. This was not the case in Asia, however, where the Stuart served on as a valuable asset of British Commonwealth and US armoured units into 1945, despite the appearance of the much more formidable M4 Sherman series. Armament consisted of the 37mm main gun and three .30cal Browning machine guns, one mounted in the hull front, one co-axial with the main gun, and one pintle-mounted on the right side of the turret, protected by a new armoured extension.

THE BLACK BEAR

T8E1 Stuart light reconnaissance vehicle

For the reconnaissance role many M5 series tanks had their turrets removed and replaced with a .50cal Browning machine gun on a ring mount. This reduced the weight and thus increased the perform- ance, and also reduced the height of its silhou- ette which made it harder to target. In the USA this conversion received the limited standard designa- tion T8E1; in the UK the M5 and M5A1 (Stuart VI) were also converted in this way. The British also used turretless Stuarts of all marks as 'Kangaroo' armoured personnel carri- ers, by fitting bench seats in the hull; and as gun tractors and armoured ambulances.

M8 Greyhound Armoured Car

Developed by the Ford Motor Co. in 1942 to fulfil a requirement for a light reconnaissance vehicle, the six-wheel-drive, rear-engined Greyhound entered service with the US Army the following year. The M8 was very fast, very quiet, and was ideally suited to its reconnaissance role. Its only shortcoming, albeit a fairly major one from the crew's point of view, was that its thin belly armour made it particularly vulnerable to mine damage. In an effort to improve protection in this area the crews would often line the floor of their vehicles with sandbags. The M8 proved to be very successful in service and production continued right up until the last month of the war, a total of 8,523 being built. Many of these vehicles continued in service with various armies long after the end of the war; numbers were still in action with the French Army in Algeria in the early 1960s.

The Greyhound served with the US Cavalry armoured reconnaissance squadrons and troops within armoured and infantry divisions; this particular M8 bears the markings of the 13th vehicle in Co.C, 82nd Reconnaissance Squadron, 2nd Armored Division in NW Europe, 1944.

The Greyhound was powered by a Hercules JXD 6-cylinder petrol engine producing 110bhp; weighing 7.5 tons, it had a maximum road speed of 56 miles per hour. Armour protection was to a maximum of 25mm; armament consisted of a 37mm main gun, a co-axial .30cal machine gun and, often, an additional ring- or pintle-mounted .50cal Browning. Overall dimensions were: length, 16ft 5ins; width, 8ft 4ins; and height, 7 feet 5 inches. The crew consisted of four men. The same chassis and hull were used for the similar turretless M20 scout and command car, armed with a .50cal on a large, raised skate ring.

(Above, left & opposite top) **Looking down, forward and left into the driver's position.**

(Opposite) **Looking down and right from the turret top.**

(Left) Looking backwards and left across the turret, from the commander's to the gunner's position. Note the turret traverse scale, the stowed 37mm ammunition, the seats attached to the turret ring, and the shield at the rear of the gun breech.

(Right) Looking forwards and right, from the gunner's to the commander's position. Note at left the telescope sight and gun elevation wheel. The ammunition feed for the co-axial machine gun passes across the top of the main gun from left to right.

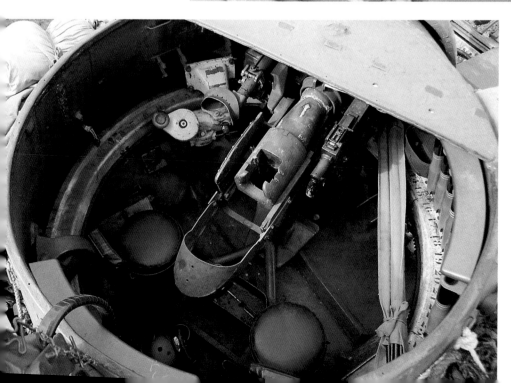

(Left) Detail of the gunner's position, with traverse control. The shield at the rear of the gun breech caught extracted shell cases and deflected them down into a container which would have been attached under the breech.

M18 Gun Motor Carriage ('Hellcat')

In December 1941 the US Ordnance Department recommended the development of a light, tracked tank-destroyer. At that time doctrine called for the tanks of the armoured divisions to be deployed primarily as 'breakthrough' weapons, fighting alongside their infantry to exploit any rupture achieved in the enemy front line. The destruction of enemy tanks was mainly to be the business of anti-tank guns, both towed and self-propelled; the latter were termed 'tank-destroyers', and assembled in battalions for attachment to other troops as required. In practice - and unsurprisingly - this tactical vision proved optimistic. The tank-destroyers were often not available where and when they were needed; and reliance on them to deal with the Panzers slowed down the improvement of conventional tank armament.

The original specification called for a 37mm gun mounted on a chassis using Christie-type suspension, and fitted with a Wright Continental R-975 radial engine. Armour protection was to be minimal in order to ensure good mobility; two prototypes were constructed, the first being completed in mid-1942. Testing of the prototype, and intelligence garnered from British combat experience in the North African desert, led to major changes in the specification. The Christie suspension was replaced by a torsion bar design, and the 37mm main gun was replaced by a series of successively larger weapons including the 57mm M1, and the 75mm M3 (mounted in a new turret on the second pilot model). Eventually, in February 1943, the Tank Destroyer Command suggested the adoption of the 76mm M1 gun which was under development for fitting to an improved model of the M4 Sherman series. Six more prototypes, designated T70 Gun Motor Carriage, were duly constructed with this

weapon. Testing resulted in a few further changes, including a simplified shape to the hull front and a new turret design with a rear 'bustle' to house a counterweight and a stowage bin. With these changes the T70 was ordered into production, and work commenced in July 1943 at the Buick factory. The vehicle received the standardised designation M18 GMC in February 1944, but in service it soon acquired the unofficial name 'Hellcat'. Production of the M18 continued until October 1944, by which time 2,507 had been built.

The Hellcat saw service mainly in Italy and NW Europe. Despite its thin armour, which made it vulnerable to the guns of late-war German Panther and Tiger tanks, it was one of the best tank-destroyers fielded by any nation. Its extremely high power-to-weight ratio made it the fastest tracked AFV of the war; this, coupled with its other virtues of low silhouette, well-sloped armour and good reliability, made it a popular vehicle with its crews. The Hellcat's superior mobility made it possible to employ the hit-and-run tactics for which the tank-destroyer had been developed, and units equipped with the M18 achieved a high tally of enemy tank 'kills' at relatively little cost to themselves.

The M18 was fitted with a Continental R-975 400bhp radial engine giving a maximum speed of 55mph; weight was 18.25 tons and maximum armour thickness 12mm. Armament comprised a 76mm M1 main gun, firing the new and very effective tungsten carbide High Velocity Armor Piercing (HVAP) ammunition; and one ring-mounted .50cal Browning machine gun. Overall dimensions were: length, 17ft 10ins (21ft 10ins including gun); width, 9ft 5in; height, 8 feet 5 inches. The Hellcat had a maximum range of 105 miles, and carried a crew of five.

(Above) Drive sprocket and torsion bar suspension.

(Left) Road wheels, track return roller and idler wheel.

(Top) Left side of turret.

(Below) Driver's position in left hull front, looking forward.

(Right) Looking down and backwards into the turret. Open-top turrets were a feature of all US tank-destroyers. They had the advantages of excellent visibility, and fast access and exit; but they left the crew dangerously vulnerable to artillery fire and infantry attack.

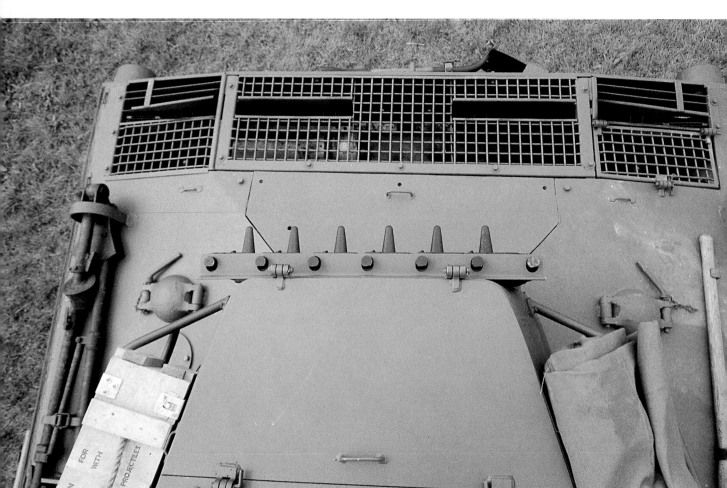

(Opposite) Looking backwards across the turret top; and the turret bustle and rear deck, looking backwards and down from the turret.

(Right & below) Looking down and forwards into the turret; and the gunner's controls on the left side of the gun breech. Note that the M1 76mm gun was only fitted into this turret by tilting the breech sideways - a feature of a number of Allied and Axis tank-destroyers produced during World War II by marrying existing guns and vehicles which were never designed to be combined.

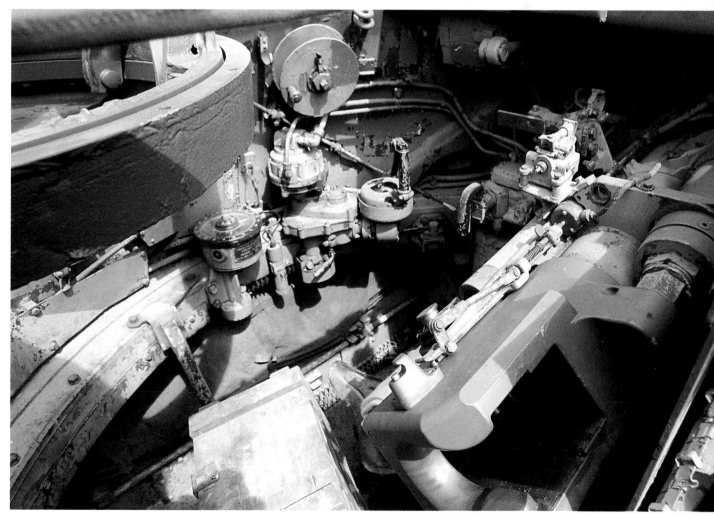

Mack NO
Truck, 7½-ton, 6x6, prime mover

The Mack NO series was the main wheeled gun tractor built for the US Army during the war, and was intended primarily to tow the 155mm gun and 8in howitzer. Production began in 1940 with the Mack NO-1 after acceptance trials of the pilot model NQ; this prototype differed from the production model in having a hard-top cab and a different type of front winch. The series progressed through successively improved models NO-2, -3, -6, and -7 during the course of the war (-4 and -5 were experimental wreckers). These vehicles were also supplied to the British Army.

Trucks of 4 tons and above were classed as 'heavy-heavy' in the US, and the Mack NO was fairly typical of the design of this class of vehicle. The only unusual aspect of the design was that in the front driven axle the usual universal joint was dispensed with in favour of a bevelled double gear reduction in the axle ends, which allowed for both driving and steering. As a result the axle housing was higher than the wheel hubs, providing extra ground clearance. Visible at the back of the truck is a yoke attached to the rear of the chassis and body which carries a chain hoist to lift the heavy trail of the gun when attaching the limber wheels for towing.

The Mack NO was fitted with a Mack EY 6-cylinder engine producing 159 brake horsepower. Overall dimensions were: length, 24ft 9ins; width, 8ft 7ins; height, 10ft 4ins (7ft 10ins minus the tilt). The vehicle's weight was 14.5 tons.

M1 155mm Howitzer

Due to excessive bureaucracy and Congressional underfunding the US Army's inventory of artillery was in a sorry state when World War I broke out in 1914; and when America entered the war three years later she was forced to obtain most of her artillery 'off the shelf' from Britain and France. After the war budgets were again severely restricted; nevertheless a lot of work was carried out during the 1920s to perfect the designs of a new generation of guns to replace those bought in during the Great War. When war threatened again in 1940 these designs were ready to be put into production with minimal delay, and by 1943 all of the World War I designs had been replaced in front-line service. One of the most important products of this development programme was the 155mm M1 howitzer, introduced in 1943 to replace the M1917. A robust, reliable weapon, the 155mm became one of the mainstays of the field artillery regiments; usually one battalion was deployed alongside three battalions of 105mm howitzers in each division. It was also fitted to several self-propelled mountings; and is still in use with many armies throughout the world today. The 155mm howitzer M1 has a maximum elevation of 63 degrees, a traverse of 50 degrees, and fires a 95lb shell to a maximum range of 9.3 miles. Weight in action is 5.7 tons.

Morris Commercial C8/AT
Tractor, 4x4, anti-tank (17pdr)

During the mid-1930s the British War Office issued a request for manufacturers of 15cwt 4x2 infantry trucks to develop all-wheel-drive versions for use as artillery tractors. The first to be developed was Guy Motors' Quad-Ant, which entered production in 1938. This was closely followed by the Morris vehicle, the Field Artillery Tractor, 4x4, Morris C8. The C8 was a four-wheel-drive derivative of the Morris Commercial CS8; with a fully enclosed steel body designed specifically for the field artillery tractor role it was a significant improvement over previous tractors. The C8 chassis was also used for other types of body including: general service, a self-propelled Bofors 40mm AA gun platform, a predictor vehicle for use in conjunction with the self-propelled Bofors, and a 2pdr portee. It was these last two types which - becoming obsolete due to advances in military technology - became surplus to requirements at about the time that the powerful new British 17-pounder towed anti-tank gun was entering service. The predictor and portee vehicles were rebuilt as tractors for the 17pdr; the conversion involved the fitting of a GS type body, providing accommodation for the seven-man gun crew plus the driver, and stowage for ammunition and associated equipment.

The C8/AT was powered by a 4-cylinder petrol engine producing 70 brake horsepower. Its overall dimensions were: length, 14ft 3ins; width, 7ft 3ins; height, 9ft; loaded weight was 4.95 tons. The example shown is a predictor-based vehicle, and is designated C8/P. The serial '46' on a Royal Artillery red/blue flash identified the anti-tank regiment within an infantry division; this truck is marked with the yellow on blue wyvern of 43rd (Wessex) Infantry Division in NW Europe, 1944-45.

(Left & below) **Morris Commercial CD/SW**

(Opposite) **Morris Commercial CS8**

Morris Commercial CD/SW

Tractor, 6x4, light anti-aircraft

The Morris Commercial CD/SW first entered service in 1937 and was a direct development of the model CD of 1932. Its appearance, however, was vastly different, as it was fitted with a lightweight cut-away bonnet to meet War Office requirements and a completely new artillery body. The vehicle had no doors, weather protection being provided by canvas side screens. The cab and body both had soft tops, and the overall height of the vehicle could be reduced to just 6ft 7ins with the tilts and windscreen folded. The original role of the CD/SW was as a tractor for 18- or 25-pounder field guns and limbers, and it was used extensively by Australian and New Zealand artillery regiments as well as those of the British Army. It was superseded by the introduction of the four-wheel-drive Quad artillery tractors, and was used instead as a tractor for the Bofors 40mm light AA gun (see pages 19-21). In this role the CD/SW carried 192 rounds of ammunition in external lockers, a spare wheel for the gun and a replacement gun barrel. The body also provided accommodation for the five-man gun crew. The CD/SW was also produced as a lightweight breakdown truck with a special body mounting a jib with a 1-ton hoist. It was powered by a 6-cylinder petrol engine producing 60bhp, and its overall dimensions were: length, 17ft 2.5ins; width, 7ft 4ins; height, 7ft 6ins (6ft 7ins with tilts folded).

Morris Commercial CS8

Truck, 15-cwt, 4x2, GS

The design of the 15-cwt WD-type infantry truck had evolved in the early 1930s, and in 1934 Morris started series production. Two years later Guy Motors started producing the Ant; and they were followed by Bedford, Commer and Ford, with Canadian production of models from Ford, GM, Chrysler and Dodge coming online from 1940. The total number of 15-cwt trucks from all manufacturers in service with British forces was over 230,000 by the end of the war. The CS8, in common with most of the other makes, was fitted with several special body types including those designated Water Tank, Office, Fitted For Wireless, Wireless (House Type), Air Compressor and Tractor. It was powered by a 6-cylinder petrol engine producing 60bhp. Dimensions were: length, 13ft 10.5ins; width, 6ft 6ins; height, 6 feet 6 inches. It weighed 1.9 tons. The example shown represents a vehicle of the British Expeditionary Force in France in 1939, finished in an early field brown scheme.

Norton 633 'Big Four'
Motorcycle combination, 3x2

Throughout the war the Norton Big Four outfit remained the only British military model to offer a sidecar wheel-drive. Based on the well-established trials model of the late 1930s, it incorporated several modifications to suit it for military service. The military pattern Norton was provided with a shaft running directly from the rear wheel, and a simple dog clutch which was engaged by a left-hand lever when additional drive was required. The frame and rear forks were modified to accommodate the extra bearings. All three wheels were interchangeable and were fitted with 4in cross-country tyres for increased traction. The sidecar was a fairly basic construction consisting of a tubular steel frame to which were attached a large protective front panel and a seat, with a wooden stowage box at the rear. Provision was also made for mounting a .303in Bren light machine gun on the sidecar. The whole sidecar body could be replaced with a platform carrying a mortar and tripod and two boxes of ammunition. The combination was provided with numerous grab handles to facilitate manhandling should it become bogged. Several thousand Big Four combinations were produced, and saw widespread use for reconnaissance and personal transport in most theatres.

The Norton 633 was powered by a Norton single-cylinder L-C-A, 633cc, 14.5hp engine, and weighed 679lbs empty and 1,232lbs fully loaded. Maximum speed was 56mph, and overall dimensions were: length, 7ft 2ins; width, 5ft 6.5ins; height, 3 feet 10.5 inches. The example shown bears the markings of a battalion of the Northumberland Fusiliers, serving with the BEF in France in 1939.

Sexton 25-pdr Self-Propelled Gun

With the build-up of British armoured strength from 1942 onwards there was increasing emphasis on providing self-propelled artillery weapons, so as to improve the armoured division's ability to operate as self-sufficiently as possible with supporting assets capable (to some degree) of accompanying the tank regiments in the advance. The Sexton was designed in 1942 in response to a British General Staff requirement for a vehicle comparable to the US M7 Priest in mobility and operational effectiveness, but mounting the British 25-pdr field gun in place of the American 105mm howitzer.

The vehicle selected to form the basis of the new design was the Canadian 'Ram', itself based on the US M3 Lee/Grant medium tank; the Ram was obsolete as a battle tank and the chassis were available for other applications. Layout was similar to the M7, but the driver's position was on the right, with the gun offset to the left. A small ammunition loading hatch was provided in the left side of the hull; and the Sexton lacked the distinctive 'pulpit' for the AA machine gun which characterised the M7.

Production commenced in early 1943 at Montreal Locomotive Works, and by the end of the year 424 vehicles had been built. Follow-up orders kept the vehicle in production until the end of 1945 and brought the total number to 2,150.

The original chassis was identical to the Ram and

(Left) **M4-type bogie with trailing return roller, road wheels and drive sprocket, seen from rear.**

(Below) **Bogie, road wheels and idler, seen from front.**

Rear hull and engine access doors.

(Above) **Rear engine deck, looking back from fighting compartment.**

(Right) **Gunner's position left of the breech.**

(Opposite top) **Fighting compartment, looking from right to left.**

(Opposite bottom) **Driver's position right of the breech. The standard 25-pdr gun/howitzer was mounted, but its recoil had to be restricted in order to prevent the breech striking the floor of the vehicle when fired at high elevations.**

the upper hull was of welded construction. Changes introduced during production included a one-piece cast nose like that of the late model Shermans, M4 type suspension bogies with trailing return rollers, a towing hook for an ammunition trailer, an auxiliary generator, increased stowage, and AA machine gun mounts. As intended, Sextons replaced the M7 Priest in one field regiment of each armoured division as they became available, and by mid-1944 had almost entirely replaced the Priest in British service. The Sexton was successful in operation and well-liked by its crews; it continued in service in Britain and Canada long after the war.

The Sexton was fitted with a Continental R-975 air-cooled radial engine producing 400bhp. Maximum speed was 25mph on the road and 20mph cross-country. The Sexton carried a crew of six; its overall dimensions were: length, 20ft 1in; width, 9ft; height, 8 feet. Armament consisted of the 25-pdr howitzer Mk II, and two .303in Bren light machine guns could be fitted for AA and infantry defence.

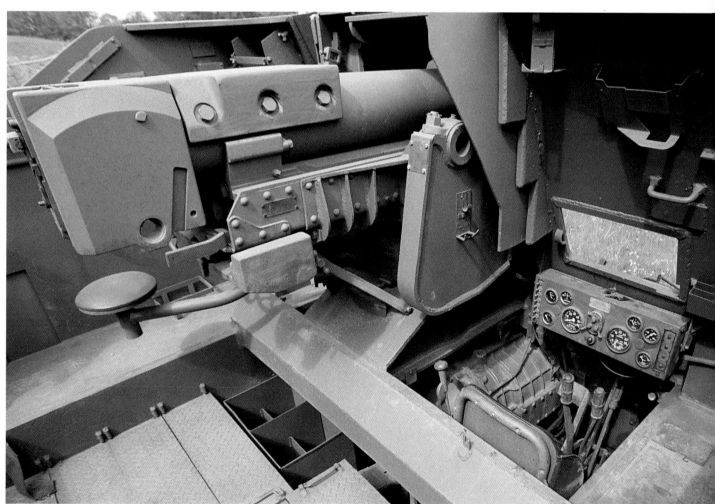

T-34/85 Model 1944

The T-34 - generally recognised as the outstanding tank of the war - was developed by Mikhail Koshkin's design team at the Kharkov Locomotive Works as a replacement for the BT series. Incorporating features from several experimental vehicles, the new design provided an excellent balance between mobility, protection and firepower. Like the BT series, the T-34 employed Christie-type suspension with full-height, paired, rubber-tyred road wheels; its broad tracks gave excellent floatation, and a ground pressure of only about 9 pounds per square inch (as against the 14psi of the M4 Sherman). The upper hull projected out on either side almost to the full width of the tracks. This facilitated what was probably the most important feature of the design - the use of heavily sloped armour to throw off enemy shells. The first production T-34s, armed with a 76.2mm gun in a two-man turret, entered mass production in 1940. Amid the ruinous defeats of the Red Army in summer 1941 the relatively few T-34 units made a notable impact; and in the counter-offensive of winter 1941-42 their superiority over the German PzKw IIIs and IVs was obvious. The T-34 was directly responsible for the German instigation of a crash programme to develop the PzKw V Panther - the first German tank to employ sloped armour.

The T-34/76 remained in production until the spring of 1945, but after the shock of their first encounter the Germans naturally took steps to redress the balance. In summer 1943, with new, more heavily armed and armoured Panzers reaching the battlefield, it was decided to redesign the T-34 to mount a more powerful 85mm gun, and the first prototypes were completed that December. The new model retained the original hull but was equipped with a completely new three-man turret; a major weakness of the T-34/76 had been

that the commander had to double as the gunner. Unfortunately the turret had been designed to accept the D-5T gun, as used in the SU-85 tank-destroyer, and was not suitable for the new ZIS-S-53 gun which had been selected for the new tank due to its superior performance. As an interim measure the first T-34/85s were produced using the old D-5T gun until the ZIS-S-53 could be re-engineered to fit the new turret. Eventually it supplanted the D-5T in the T-34/85 Model 1944 in spring 1944.

The opportunity was also taken to make further changes to the turret. The commander's cupola was moved further aft to allow more room for the gunner; and the radio was moved from the co-driver's position up to the turret so that the commander had more control over it. In this form the T-34 reached its ultimate development, and is thought by many to have been - on a balance of mobility, firepower, protection, reliability and ease of mass production - the most efficient tank produced by any nation during the war. It was crude, noisy, and uncomfortable - but mechanically dependable, simple to maintain, tough, and very hard-hitting. At least 40,000 T-34s were built during the war, and probably as many after it - they soldiered on in many of the USSR's client armies into the 1970s, and hold the record for the longest service career of any tank in history.

The Model 1944 was powered by a V2 V-12 liquid-cooled diesel engine producing 500bhp. Maximum road speed was 34mph and weight was 31.4 tons. Armour protection was to a maximum of 90mm and armament consisted of an 85mm ZIS-S-53 main gun and two 7.62mm DT machine guns; it had a crew of five. Overall dimensions were: length, 26ft 8ins; width, 9ft 10ins; height, 8 feet 6 inches.

(Above) Looking down and forward from the commander's cupola, towards the gunner's station on the left of the gun breech.

(Right) The turret roof, with commander's cupola (left) and loader's hatch.

(Opposite top left) The massive driver's hatch in the glacis offers both access, and good visibility when driving 'opened up'; when the hatch was closed for combat the inset periscopes gave as poor visibility as in any tank of the period.

(Opposite top right) Driver's seat and left wall of the forward compartment. Most of the main gun ammunition was carried in the steel cases forming the floor of the fighting compartment.

(Opposite) The driver's (left) and co-driver/hull machine gunner's positions in the forward compartment; this was fairly roomy, but had limited headroom. Steering the T-34 across country, by means of the conventional left and right track control levers, notoriously required long arms and brute strength.

(Above) Left side of the turret with radio and commander's flip-up seat.

(Right) The simple but efficient gunner's controls and telescopic sight on the left side of the massive breech of the ZIS-S-53 gun.

Turret roof interior, looking upwards at the hatch
of the commander's
cupola.

Loader's position on the
right of the gun breech,
with the co-axial machine
gun and stowed maga-
zines.

Windsor Carrier (T16)

The original role envisaged for the British Army's Universal carrier was as a fast, lightly armoured vehicle to carry infantry across ground denied by small-arms fire. A specific task was to transport Bren light machine guns and their teams, in a reconnaissance and intervention platoon within the headquarters company of the infantry battalion - hence the common name 'Bren gun carrier' for the whole family of vehicles, although this was just one of the many versions. In fact all the numerous variants produced were properly known as the Universal carrier. Over 40,000 were built in the UK, some 29,000 in Canada, and a modified version in Australia and New Zealand.

Meanwhile it was decided that a slightly larger version of this versatile vehicle was desirable for tasks that required a greater capacity. The new carrier was longer than the Universal, having an additional road wheel on each side, and was fitted with a more powerful engine. The new vehicle was known as the Windsor carrier; 5,000 were built in Canada and 14,000 in the USA, where it was known as the T16.

The hulls of these vehicles comprised a simple steel box with a motor compartment situated in the centre. In front at the right sat a driver, and alongside him a gunner (the Bren was the usual weapon in both types, but in the first half of the war some Universals also mounted the .55in Boyes anti-tank rifle). The radiator was mounted in a bulkhead between them, and the noise generated by the fan effectively drowned out any conversation between the crew, as vehicles of this type were not fitted with any form of internal communications.

Behind the two crew were two rectangular compartments, one each side of the engine, which accomodated a variety of stores and/or personnel (under the most spartan and uncomfortable conditions). Loads varied, and it was common to find both types of carrier employed in a number of roles, e.g. carrying ammunition, rations and stores of all kinds in the front lines; casualty evacuation; carrying infantry support weapons such as medium mortars (81 mm) and medium machine guns (usually the .303in Vickers); and towing anti-tank guns and trailers. Because it was fully tracked the carrier proved to be a reasonably good cross-country vehicle, and it was both agile and very fast for its time. The controls of the Windsor differed from those of the Universal carrier, the Windsor being fitted with the more usual brake lever steering in place of the unique track-bowing system of the Universal. The crew varied between two and five men depending on the role.

Overall dimensions were: length, 12ft 4ins; width, 6ft 9ins; height, 5 feet 3 inches. The vehicle was fitted with a Ford V8 95/100hp water-cooled petrol engine; and maximum armour thickness was 12mm. Maximum road speed was 31mph, and range was 159 miles.

This example bears the sign of 8th Armoured Brigade; the serial '1177' on the Royal Artillery flash identifyies 147th Field Regiment (Essex Yeomanry).

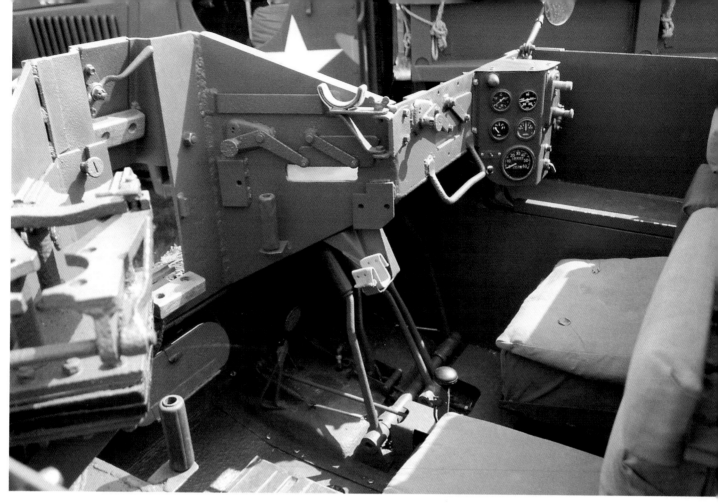

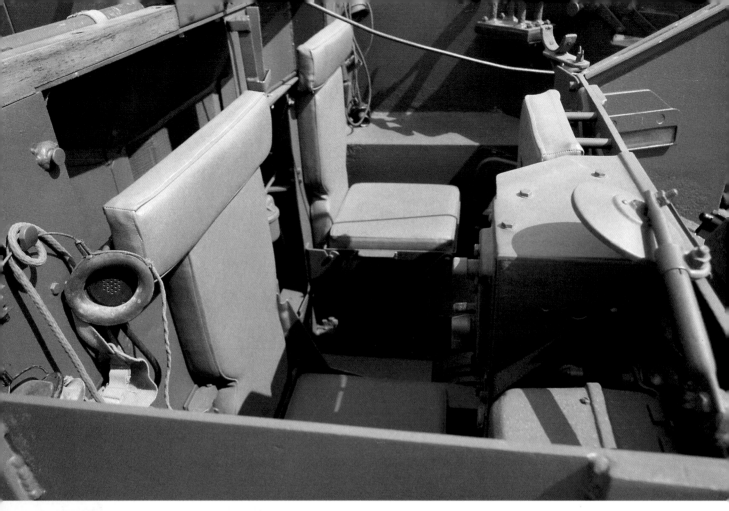

Ward LaFrance Model 1000

Truck, 6-ton, 6x6, heavy wrecker (M1)

The common layout for US military trucks had been established in the 1930s, and the favoured design was a normal control (long bonnet) truck with, in most cases, six-wheel-drive; dual rear wheels were the norm. Load capacity was usually underquoted to allow a large overload in emergencies; a huge range of such trucks were produced in nominal capacities ranging from 2½ tons to 12 tons. The heavier trucks often filled the role of tractors for artillery or, in some cases, tank transporters. One such heavy duty six-wheeled truck was built by Ward LaFrance and, unusually, only a recovery variant appeared.

The first type, the M1, used a civilian pattern sheet metal cab, but a later version, the M1A1, had an open cab with folding canvas top. Production of the M1A1 was shared between Ward LaFrance and Kenworth. The US forces and the British Army used both variants, the early versions serving mostly with the British Army in the Middle East and Italy. Most were provided under the terms of the Lend-Lease agreement. The powerful main winch and power-operated lifting crane made the Ward LaFrance a very capable recovery vehicle much favoured by those who used it.

The Truck, Heavy Wrecker, 6-ton, 6x6, M1 (Ward La France Model 1000) was powered by a Continental 22R 6-cylinder engine, producing 145bhp. Overall dimensions were: length, 26ft 6ins; width, 8ft 3ins; height, 10ft 2ins; the weight was 25.2 tons. The example shown is the earlier version, the M1 Wrecker.